TEWKESBURY
REVISITED

TEWKESBURY
REVISITED

CLIFF BURD

TEMPUS

Frontispiece: Tewkesbury High Street from The Cross at the turn of the twentieth century. Gas lamps are in use and the only traffic is that of local delivery horses and carts. This scene has changed very little since that date: the majority of the buildings remain the same, just the names of the new owners being different.

First published 2005

Tempus Publishing Limited
The Mill, Brimscombe Port,
Stroud, Gloucestershire, GL5 2QG
www.tempus-publishing.com

British Library Cataloguing in Publication Data.
A catalogue record for this book is available from the British Library.

ISBN 0 7524 3476 4

Typesetting and origination by Tempus Publishing Limited.
Printed in Great Britain.

Contents

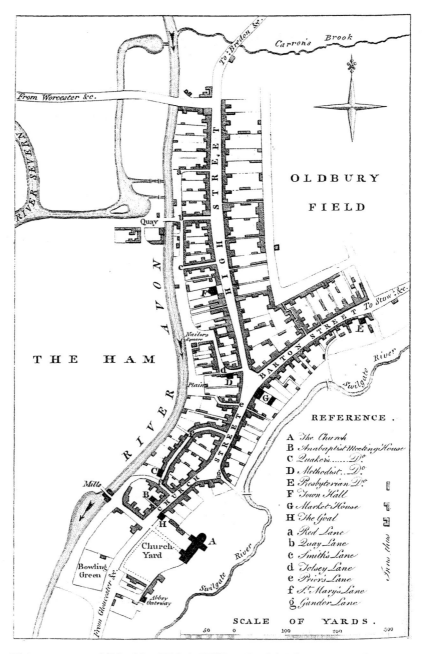

REFERENCE.

A   The Church
B   Anabaptist Meeting House
C   Quaker's ...... Dº
D   Methodist .. Dº
E   Presbyterian Dº
F   Town Hall
G   Market House
H   The Goal

a   Red Lane
b   Quay Lane
c   Smith's Lane
d   Tolsey Lane
e   Prior's Lane
f   Sᵗ Mary's Lane
g   Gander Lane

SCALE   OF   YARDS.

This map was published in 1793, in William Dyde's *The History and Antiquities of Tewkesbury*, the first of three editions. There was a list of subscribers totalling 121 names, a surpassingly high number for this kind of local publication. In the preface to the second edition he wrote, 'when success stimulates to new exertions, and gratitude displays itself in a solicitude to please, the public, it is hoped, will allow that favour has not been misplaced, or encouragement thrown away' – the language of the age!

Acknowledgements

The contents of this book are a result of many years of collecting, rummaging and begging of postcards, photographs and other ephemera. I would like to place on record my gratitude to the many people who have sent me pictures and information, names and places, to give the images life and character. There are a few who have tremendous recall, and to Mrs Edna Fletcher, a lady of advanced years, my thanks for names and places. To others: Barry Sweet, Mary Avery, Tewkesbury Borough Museum, Marian Poole, John Dixon, P. Fisher, Josie and Mike Parsons, Margaret Gittins and the many who have allowed me to use their material. Finally, my thanks to my wife Pat, whose patience and support continues to surprise me and without whom the book would not have been completed.

Introduction

The location of Tewkesbury, standing as it does on a spit of gravel and surrounded by two major rivers – the Severn and the Avon – and several smaller streams, has to a great extent formulated its shape and its size. The architects of the abbey realised that the land would be subject to flooding and consequently built this wonderful edifice on one of the higher parts of the land available. Further development took place outside the abbey walls, with properties being erected at some distance from the rivers but generally running parallel, these waterways being the commercial highways between the town and the surrounding country. As these frontages were gradually built up, and the surrounding land was subject to flooding, the only course of action left for development was to build at right angles to the main streets. The result, of course, was the development of the alleyways.

The movement of people away from the land and into the towns and cities during the early part of the nineteenth century gave rise to the development of back-to-back housing, rows of tenements and, in towns like Tewkesbury, two- and three-storey housing in the alleys and courts. The population of the town rose during the period 1800–51 from 4,800 to 5,600, an enormous rise for such a small town.

The result of this population increase, considering the lack of fresh water, no sewage disposal and the close confines within the alleys, was a high mortality rate. Diseases such as cholera ran their course through the town at intervals; the only action that the local authority could take was to burn all the bedding in the house and whitewash the walls. All the waste products were washed into a series of channels running from the streets and into the several watercourses in the town. The fact that there was no running water meant that, if there was no well serving the area, water would be obtained in buckets from the Avon or the Swilgate Brook. Little wonder then that cholera ran through Tewkesbury, taking the lives of young and old without favour. These hardships, the poverty, disease and the close living conditions, all contributed to the formation of the character of the people.

Industry in the nineteenth century was limited. The stocking-knitting trade gave employment to upwards of 1,000 people, working from their homes for the Master Hosiers. The river with its trade to and from Bristol, Gloucester and Worcester, carrying grain, coal and many other goods, made Tewkesbury a busy active inland port. Nailmaking flourished for a time, with some of this being carried on in the homes of residents. The tanning of leather and associated industries such as boot- and shoemaking were also prevalent in the 1800s, as is witnessed by the Tanners' Arms public house in St Mary's Lane. The various census returns show many residents obtaining a living from the rivers, as bargemen, ropemakers and the like. There were some small engineering firms, the most famous being Walkers, who were involved in the manufacture of fairground equipment. It was only after the Second World War that industry came to the town, with several large employers building factories near the town.

The Industrial Revolution, however, bypassed the town to a great extent but the stagecoaches brought business here in the form of Post Houses and the stabling and provisioning of horses. At its heyday, there were upwards of thirty coaches each day stopping in the town, on their way to the Midlands and Wales. We should consider it a blessing that the town was bypassed, as the town retained many of its finest buildings and the alleyways so typical of the place.

The Second World War brought some employment as a result of the development of an army camp on its outskirts. Ashchurch camp became a base for American forces and provided work not only for those civilians working on the base but also for those providing services in the town. After the war, the Americans left and the camp became a workshop for the British Army, with several hundred soldiers being stationed there.

Later, a great deal of engineering firms used the area as a source of labour, with several large companies being built in the environs of Tewkesbury. Meanwhile, the advent of the M5 motorway has increased Tewkesbury's importance as a distribution centre, with large tracts of land given over to warehousing.

In 1971, the town celebrated the 850th anniversary of the consecration of the abbey and the 500th anniversary of the Battle of Tewkesbury with a summer-long festival. To crown the year, the Queen visited the town to distribute Maundy money at the abbey.

The town, which is now part of a much larger local authority, has much to offer: with the rivers, the abbey and a fine townscape, it is one of the finest of the nation's country towns.

Cliff Burd

November 2004

one

People

Tewkesbury is a comparatively small community – only recently has the town developed to its present size of population – and it has always had a good community spirit. Through many generations, adversity and hardship have forged bonds between the families. The multitude of organisations which have sprung up have brought about friendly, and sometimes not so friendly, rivalry between the members. This chapter is a small indication of the diversity of activities and organisations in this little country town.

This is the Nelson Street 1945 Party. The end of hostilities in Europe was the signal for celebrations all across the country. This is just one of the many street parties to be held in the town. The Mums and Dads are lined up at the rear and include Mrs Chamberlain, Gwen Cull, Mrs. Lampitt, Mrs Mellor, D. Hartell and Mr and Mrs Cumberlin. The children include Val Gyngell, Alf Cumberlin, Pat Parsons, Gwen Hopton, John Lampitt, Doreen Taylor, Bunty Liddel, Billy Hooper, Christine Booth, M. Else, T. Lampitt and M.Hemming.

The St John's Ambulance Brigade has a long tradition of service to the community, attending the many sporting and social functions without any thought of reward. Here we can see the annual visit of the County Officer on a tour of inspection. From left to right: the County Officer, Stan Ricketts, (who ran this body for over thirty years), Henry Ricketts, Rex Bishop, –?–, –?– and Francis Sears. The headquarters were situated in Post Office Lane.

Left: Brian and Edna Linnel show off their Dickensian costumes at a Tewkesbury Festival of Arts Dickens Day in around 1980. They were just two of over fifty people who took part. All were dressed in period costume and the town mayor, Mrs J. Potter, judged both costume and presentation. This was followed by a parade through the streets.

Below: At the election of the mayor in 1908, the illness of one of the local councillors caused an upset. The favourite candidate was Cllr W.T. Boughton (left), a businessman with a boot and shoe shop in Barton Street. Unfortunately for him, Alderman Jones was ill on the day of the election and the loss of his vote and the casting vote of the outgoing mayor meant that Cllr G.C. Bayliss (right) was elected mayor. This would be a highly unlikely occurrence in the well-organised political arena of today.

Above: Army days at Ashchurch camp in 1950, at a time when the camp was a temporary home for some 500 servicemen. It was the practice of the local photographer to take a few shots of some of the guests after a wedding. Here is a group outside the Sabrina cinema on a Saturday afternoon after a wedding at the Riverside Hotel. From left to right: Cliff Burd, Pat Gibbard, S. Staley, Sylvia Woodley, Colin Davey, Barbara Hudman, Jock Clark and and –?–.

Opposite: In around 1939, a group of young men with their whole future ahead were sitting on the window sill of the town hall when someone happened along with a camera. From left to right: two brothers called Bob and Ted Rivers, R. Halling, K. Matty, T. Ryland, H. Ricketts. In front are A. Hopton and M. Tombs, the young man standing on the far left is unknown.

The 12 December 1908 issue of the *Cheltenham Chronicle and Gloucestershire Graphic* featured the Tewkesbury Christmas Market. This was one of the major events in the year, attracting farmers and butchers from the surrounding area. The prize-winning beast would be paraded around the town before being prepared for sale at Christmas by the proud butcher who would have paid top price for the privilege of displaying the carcass.

A group of enthusiastic young anglers from the secondary modern and grammar schools about to enter a fishing competition in around 1949. The organiser from the Tewkesbury Angling Club is Ken Haines, standing third from the right, at the rear. The participants include C. Hill, G. Groves, F. Powell, ? Bennett, A. Hodges, T. Sharpe, D. Turner, S. Hooper, P. Townsend, G. Haines, D. Walker, A. Pryce Jones, A. Cromwell, B. Ryland and ? Parlour.

The Cheltenham Chronicle and Gloucestershire Graphic in January 1924 issued these pictures of the revival of miracle plays at Tewkesbury Abbey in Christmas 1923. These plays were performed in medieval times and as such are recorded in the abbey records. From left to right: J. Dudley, E. Freeman, Revd E. Hanson, Mr E. Boulton, Revd J. Mercier, H. Norman, J. Parsons, H. Healey, Revd T. Lambert, D. Taylor. Kneeling: H. Morris, W. Purser.

Here are the 'lower orders' from the same series of plays: shepherds all with crooks at the ready. From left to right: E. Hopkins, A. Custance, G. Smith, R. Newman, W. Sims, C. Hobbs, J. Jones, A. Bulled, F. Pemberton. Sitting in front: H. Purser.

Right: The Lane family, Australia, April 1958. Former Gloucester ambulance man Harold Lane, who resided in Queens Road, Priors Park, decided in 1956 to emigrate to Australia, to start a new life there. He and his wife and two sons departed to see if the grass was greener there than in Tewkesbury. He took up a post piloting a two-way-radio-linked vehicle for the Queensland Ambulance Brigade. The family settled there permanently.

Tewkesbury has an excellent record for looking after its more senior residents. This is a group from the Golden Hour Club, an organisation for those who have reached a 'certain age'. In 1962 they gathered together ready to set off on one of their regular coach outings, perhaps a tour of the Cotswolds. The mayor and mayoress, Cllr and Mrs Marston, can be seen in the centre of the group. Others include Mrs Key, Mrs Moore, Mrs Brick and Mrs Cash. The gentleman to the right of the front row is Jack Hughes. This may have been a special day, as most of them are wearing flowers.

Ashchurch Cricket Club Annual Dinner, 1961. At the long table in the centre of the photograph from left to right are: Mrs Thomas, T. King, Mr Thomas, Mrs King, Mrs Amphlett and T. Amphlett. At the top of the picture, the guests of honour are Mayor Workman and his wife.

The opening of the Dowty Ashchurch Sports and Social Club in around 1960, with Chairman George Dowty bowling the first ball down the skittle alley. He later became Sir George, receiving this accolade for his services to industry. The Dowty Group employed many thousands of local people and provided this kind of facility for their employees. Watching with interest are Bob Raven (second from right) and Mr Mace (second from left).

At No.122 High Street was this greengrocer's shop when this picture was taken in 1925. Edith Groves, later to become Mrs Watson, is second from the left with her sister Emily. They are flanked by two sisters, Kit and Bunt Sayers. The future husband of Edith, Mr Watson, operated from the shop next door as a jeweller and watchmaker.

These are members of the Dickens Fellowship, a substantial organisation for many years in the town, in around 1958. Meeting regularly at the town hall, they organised events both for members and for the general public. Here are three of the prime movers, from left to right: Mrs Robinson, Mr W. 'Toot' Gibson and Mr Nation, headmaster of Tewkesbury Secondary School.

A group of soldiers ready to do battle in 1931. This was part of a scene for the pageant held in the field at the rear of the abbey. A large number of the local population took part in the battle scenes and were expected to make their own weapons, wooden swords and their chain mail of knitted wool. It was an extremely popular event but the only soldier identifiable here is Cecil Graham, fifth from the right in the front row.

The stunning blonde standing on the left is Brian Wanklyn with his chauffeur, Howard Nash, standing by on the right

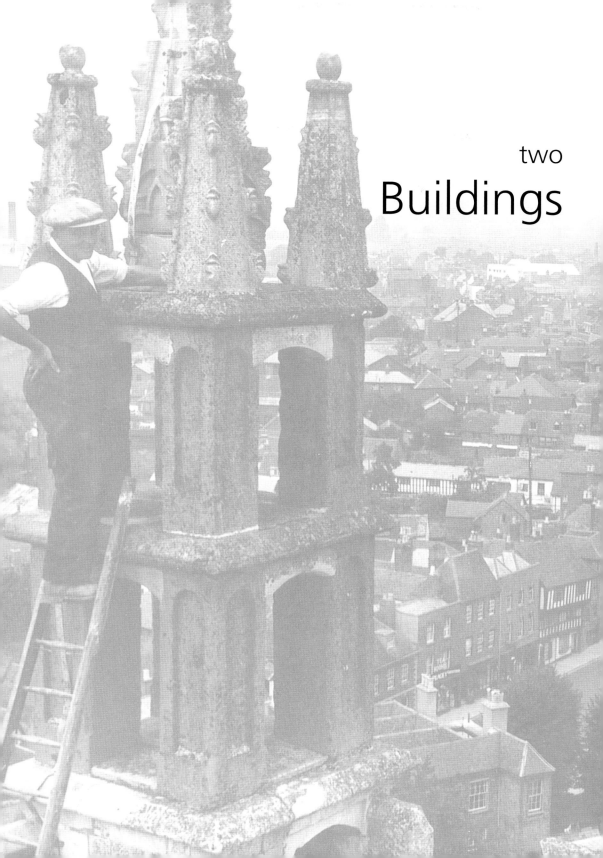

two
Buildings

With the exception of the 1965 redevelopment of the upper High Street, any time traveller from the Victorian period would recognise the three main streets of the town immediately. The mere fact that the Industrial Revolution did not take hold in Tewkesbury and the main-line railway bypassed the town was indeed the saviour of the entire fabric of the centre. The mixture of architectural styles, from timber-framed sixteenth-century through Georgian and Queen Anne to Victorian, sit well together and give the town most of its character.

Abbey Gateway. Tewkesbury.

Printed by G Rowe. Lithographer Exeter House Cheltenham.

This lithograph of the Abbey Gateway was drawn by a Cheltenham artist, George Rowe, in around 1841. It shows the substantial gateway giving access to the vicarage but the original gateway to the abbey would have been in the vicinity of The Crescent. The building lies to the west of Abbey House and is a two-storey late fifteenth-century structure once used as a prison for those in debt to the abbot. Thomas Collins restored it in 1850 and the two doors are carved oak, added just a few years later.

Shops on the north side of the High Street in 1965. These were mainly small shops, which were in need of renovation. The upper storeys were retained while the shop frontages were redesigned and brought up to date.

Each year floods hit the town, sometimes as many as four or five times during the winter. Some years are worse than others but in 1924 the town was flooded during June, an unprecedented occurrence. The road into town was almost impassable, with lorries struggling through and a Black and White bus on its way to London finding it difficult. Help was at hand in the shape of the horse and cart following along.

This is Church Street looking towards The Cross around 1906, judging by the dress. The people are out on the street and appear to be waiting for some kind of parade, perhaps the local council. There is at least one flag out too. At the right-hand side of the picture, in the background, there are two lamps standing on top of the Wesleyan Chapel gate, which the following picture shows have gone.

A different view of Church Street, some twenty years later in around 1923. This postcard records a street bazaar outside the Methodist church, perhaps to raise funds for the church. The lady standing by the railings, under the street sign, seems to be in Salvation Army dress so it may be a joint effort. The two lamps have gone from the gates now.

This stunning view of the town, as seen from the very top of the tower of Tewkesbury Abbey, was taken in 1936 as part of the publicity for an appeal to raise funds for the restoration of the tower. The man on the ladder is Jack Day, one of the builders who played a major part in the work. Sadly, a few years later Mr Day was working on a lower scaffold when he fell and lost his life. The white building in the distance is the Sabrina cinema, just built in that year.

In the early 1970s, the mills (which had belonged to Mr Rice) had been derelict for some time. These and all the ancillary buildings were demolished to make way for repair workshops for Allied Mills. The mills had been one of the larger employers for many years and were in a prime site, situated next to the river and the quay. The man on the right is Maurice Ryder.

Opposite, above: In January 1960, the *Tewkesbury Register* published this view of Barton Street. The area was to be used for a new post office at that time. However, after the demolition of these properties, which were obviously in a state of disrepair, a new police station was erected instead.

Opposite, below: This is the same site as shown in the previous photograph, with the old buildings now gone and the new police station nearing completion. To the left of the new building is Charlewood Alley, named after a tailor of that name who was living there in around 1840.

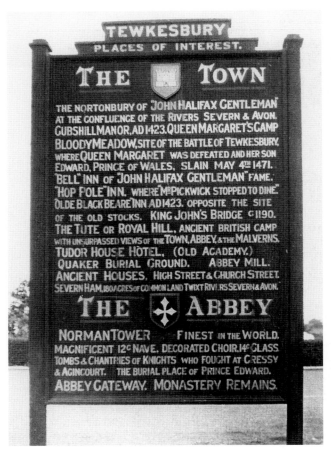

TEWKESBURY
PLACES OF INTEREST.

THE ✠ TOWN

THE NORTONBURY OF JOHN HALIFAX GENTLEMAN AT THE CONFLUENCE OF THE RIVERS SEVERN & AVON. GUBSHILL MANOR, AD 1423. QUEEN MARGARET'S CAMP. BLOODY MEADOW, SITE OF THE BATTLE OF TEWKESBURY, WHERE QUEEN MARGARET WAS DEFEATED AND HER SON EDWARD, PRINCE OF WALES, SLAIN MAY 4TH 1471. 'BELL' INN OF 'JOHN HALIFAX GENTLEMAN' FAME. 'HOP POLE' INN. WHERE 'MR PICKWICK STOPPED TO DINE.' OLDE BLACK BEARE INN AD 1423. OPPOSITE THE SITE OF THE OLD STOCKS. KING JOHN'S BRIDGE C 1190. THE TUTE OR ROYAL HILL, ANCIENT BRITISH CAMP WITH UNSURPASSED VIEWS OF THE TOWN, ABBEY, & THE MALVERNS. TUDOR HOUSE HOTEL, (OLD ACADEMY.) QUAKER BURIAL GROUND.   ABBEY MILL. ANCIENT HOUSES, HIGH STREET & CHURCH STREET. SEVERN HAM, 180 ACRES OF COMMON LAND TWIXT RIVERS SEVERN & AVON.

THE ✠ ABBEY

NORMAN TOWER   FINEST IN THE WORLD. MAGNIFICENT 12C NAVE. DECORATED CHOIR. 14C GLASS TOMBS & CHANTRIES OF KNIGHTS WHO FOUGHT AT CRESSY & AGINCOURT.   THE BURIAL PLACE OF PRINCE EDWARD. ABBEY GATEWAY. MONASTERY REMAINS.

Left: This was an information board set up by the local council to advertise all the attractions of the town. It was sited in the Gloucester Road car park, and carried the town crest at the top. It was no high-tech, illuminated press-button board but it was state of the art in 1950.

Below: This large property, which used to stand on Ashchurch Road, was the home of Leonard Hone and his family at the time of this picture around 1935. The site was cleared in the 1950s and Ald Knights School (named after Alderman Knight) was built here for children with learning difficulties. The lady at the door is the housekeeper, Mrs Wanklyn, whose husband also worked at the house. This property would be worth a great deal today.

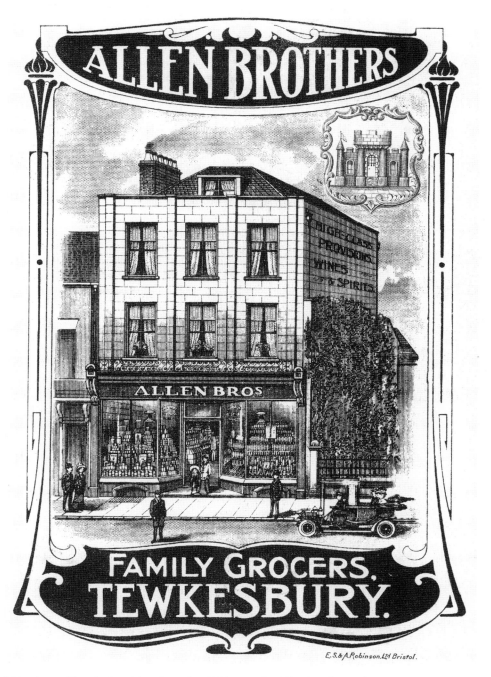

This piece of local advertising from the 1920s was for Allen Brothers, a business run by local men who attended Tewkesbury Grammar School before taking over the business from their father. The poster is typical of the period, even using the town crest in the advert.

TEWKESBURY.

FREEHOLD PROPERTY

AND

VOTES

For the Eastern Division of Gloucestershire.

To be Sold by Auction, by

PHILIP THOMAS,

On TUESDAY, the 21st day of FEBRUARY, 1854,

AT THE

King's Head Inn, Tewkesbury,

At FIVE o'Clock in the Afternoon, in lots:

By order of the Mortgagee under his powers of Sale

LOT 1.—A NEAT BRICK BUILT

COTTAGE,

With lean-to Shed, situate in Smith's Court, in the CHURCH STREET, in the occupation of THOMAS WYSE.

LOT 2.—A

BRICK BUILT COTTAGE

With lean-to Shed, adjoining Lot 1, with a Frontage to St. MARY'S LANE, in the occupation of the Widow ROWLAND.

The Tenants will, on application, shew the respective lots, and for further particulars apply to Messrs Badham & Brookes, Solicitors, or the Auctioneer, all of Tewkesbury.

This poster from 1854 advertises the auction of two cottages in Smith's Court. The first lot has a small lean-to shed and is occupied. The second lot fronts onto St Mary's Lane and is also occupied. The attraction of these properties was that the freeholder also had the privilege of the vote that went with ownership.

Wynyard House School was a small select private school at the end of Barton Road. The building was set back from the road and had been the home of a local businessman and his family. Boys were accepted as both day and boarder pupils but girls could only attend as day students. The age range was five years to eleven years and prepared students for public school and GCE examinations. It was a fairly short-lived venture, lasting only a few years during the 1960s.

A popular view of a well-known building, the Abbey Mill, this time difficult to access because of the floods in March 1947. The view shows the Ham field under water, an occurrence seen several times each winter and occasionally in the summer too.

This scene at the Black Bear at the corner of Mythe Road could be a scene from the mid-nineteenth century but was actually part of the Dickens Fellowship celebrations commemorating the 100th anniversary of *The Pickwick Papers* in July 1928. Mr W.H. Knutt, dressed in white breeches, is Mr Pickwick and the whole group drove around the town calling at the hostelries. Here Bob Milward is providing refreshments.

Opposite, above: The Abbey Mill was a working flour mill for many years, processing local grain into flour and feed for the area. This is a postcard from around 1930, showing the upper floor where the hoppers were. In the story of John Halifax, Gentleman, written by Mrs Craik, Abel Fletcher, the miller, throws the last remaining bags of flour left in the town into the river Avon, to prevent a riot. This was after a particularly bad harvest.

Opposite, below: The Abbey Mill has been reinvented as a well-appointed restaurant in this postcard view from around 1930. The overall effect is very pleasant and the mill catered for locals as well as accepting bookings from organisations across the Midlands. In the 1970s, the proprietor offered a new feature: medieval banquets, complete with a Lord of the Manor and a Court Jester.

This is an early morning view of Church Street in 1912. The streets have just been washed and some of the shop awnings are down already, so it was likely to be a warm day. Traffic is virtually non-existent, just a couple of horses and carts and the odd cyclist. Note the workman on the extreme left, painting the sign on the Plough public house.

Opposite, above: Tewkesbury railway station was situated just on the edge of town and replaced the original station on the High Street. The building, seen here in around 1925, was quite splendid and boasted a WHSmith newspaper shop. The station was on a link from Ashchurch station through Tewkesbury to Ripple and Malvern and had a goods link into town and the Allied Mills.

Opposite, below: Nelson Street was due for redevelopment around 1980. The houses and ancillary buildings were mainly early Victorian and these buildings backed onto Hunter's Court, a derelict area. The red-brick building on the left was the Salvation Army Citadel, also ready for a facelift. The houses are gone now and new properties have been built.

Martins Mill and buildings were in the Oldbury, next to the old railway lines which led down to Allied Mills. Its demolition is in full flow here, with the digger taking down the ancillary buildings. The firm of Martin, whose business was in The Oldbury, adjacent to the original railway station, was demolished after the firm closed down in the late 1960s.

Above: The Abbey Mill has always been a popular venue for visiting organisations. Coaches would pre-book a meal and the visitors would take in the sights. This is a visit of a Mothers' Union group from Worcester. The proprietor, on the left, is John Atkins. He dressed for his visitors in a bow tie and offered postcards and other goods for sale.

CORONATION ILLUMINATIONS. 22ⁿᵈ JUNE 1911. THE TOWN HALL.

Right: Tewkesbury Town Hall in all its glory, splendidly illuminated for the Coronation of King George V on 22 June 1911. The whole town celebrated, with shops closing at 1 p.m. and a service being held at the abbey. All the schoolchildren, some 1,350, paraded through the streets and then went off to their respective tea parties and received a Coronation mug each.

The business premises of Messrs Coutts and Howells in Barton Street, decorated for the Coronation in 1911. As part of the celebrations, merry-go-rounds were erected at The Cross and two free rides were given to each child. In the afternoon, Harry Hewett gave a Punch and Judy show at the Watson Hall for them, and for the adults there was dancing in Barton Street until the early hours. Later, Mayor Baker received a medal from His Majesty, with a letter signed by Winston Churchill.

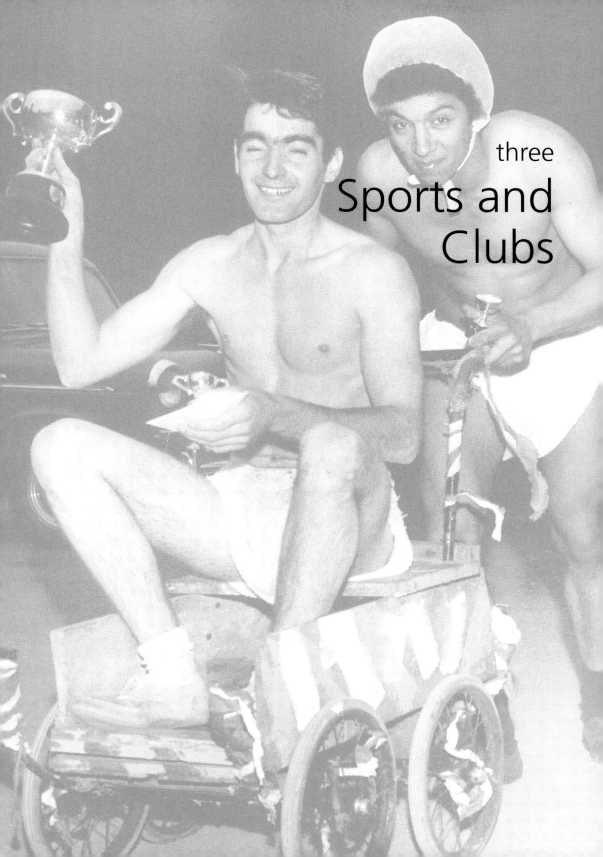

three
Sports and Clubs

During the later years of the Victorian era, many clubs sprang into being. Bearing in mind that most working men were employed for up to sixty hours per week, working six days out of seven, it is surprising that they had any real leisure time at all. Golf, cycling, bowls and several football clubs have come and gone. Others, like the cricket club and the YMCA teams have survived and thrived. Rowing was a major activity going into the twentieth century and between the wars there was a flourishing sports club, with tennis and hockey being played regularly.

For many years Tewkesbury was the destination for hundreds of visitors from Birmingham and other towns in the Midlands. With two rivers and many large open spaces, there were ample leisure opportunities in the summer for those living in large cities. This was the camping site, operated by the local council and situated in the Vineyards, an area now taken over by Tewkesbury Rugby Club.

Opposite, above: Tewkesbury has not always had its own swimming pool; originally, people swam in the rivers. In 1928 the old borough council made a small site available for swimming in the river Severn, close to the weir. Sand was deposited here, hence the name 'The Sandy'. This was where most of the locals began swimming. There were huts for changing and an enclosed paddling area. Taking a giant leap forward, the local council built this small outdoor pool, known as the Bird Bath, at the Gloucester Road car park, specifically for schoolchildren. This is the formal opening, with the mayor and several councillors present, in around 1960.

Above: Tewkesbury has had its tennis enthusiasts for many years and this facility, shown here in around 1960, was built at the same site as the Bird Bath. This was the only hard court in the town, but there were grass courts at the Swilgate Cricket Club in Gander Lane.

Known locally as the Moats, probably because of the land's association with the abbey, this is the area now developed as Despenser Road. The children of Wenlock Road, led by Mr Messenger, are taking advantage of the severe winter of 1963. Not only sledges were used but also tin trays and anything else which would slide.

Opposite, above: The game of skittles – ninepin rather than the American style – has been popular in the town for more than 100 years. Each pub of any consequence had its own alley and its own team. There were local and district leagues and it is only in recent years that the sport has died away. This alley was at the George, a pub at the top of the High Street, which recently lost its way and became a small nightclub but is now back to its normal state.

Opposite, below: This splendid body of young women is the Tewkesbury High School hockey team, shown here on the Swilgate ground in around 1930. The high school itself backed onto this ground, which was used as a sporting venue for most of the local schools as well as the cricket and hockey clubs.

The Tewkesbury Grammar School football squad pose outside one of the classrooms in the Church Street building in 1914. These were the sons of local farmers and businessmen, expected to carry on from their fathers. Two of the boys second and third from the left in the back row are the Allen brothers, who took over the grocery business shown in the advertisement in Chapter Two.

A new sport emerged in Tewkesbury in the early 1960s: hoseball. This event was introduced and organised by the local fire station and the officers there. It took place on the Vineyards field behind the abbey, usually on a bank holiday weekend. Spectators had to be careful not to get too close!

Another event from around 1960 was the Pram Race. Competitors, dressed in suitable fashion in nappies and bonnets, sat in a pram for the journey. The principle was to race through the town, stopping at each pub to drink half a pint and then racing to the next pub. On the extreme left are George Jordan and bearded baby Ivor Munn, while the pair third from left are Dave Hallings and Neville Nash.

The Swimming Club Gala of 1932 took place at the Quay, beyond the mills and the area where barges loaded and unloaded from the river. The scene shows that the sport was very popular. Spectators are not only taking up the whole of the bank area but are sitting on top of the goods wagons used by the mill for delivery. A float has been erected for contestants and officials. All this took place at a time when the only swimming facility was the river.

Opposite: Here are the winning team: Neville Nash in the pram with the pusher Dave Hallings. The judges could never be certain how many drinks had been taken during these races and there was a good deal of nobbling on the circuit!

Above: Tewkesbury was for many years a centre for rowing. The Tewkesbury Regatta was a national event, drawing teams from across the country. It should be no surprise therefore that the town boasted a strong rowing club. Here they are competing at an annual event at the Worcester College for the Blind in July 1924, on the river Severn, with the club secretary, Mr Watson, on the right.

Norman Jackson, landlord of the Barrel pub in the High Street, is handing a trophy to the captain of the winning darts team in 1960. From left to right: Dave Hill, -?-, Norman Jackson, John Watson, -?-, Alf Crisp and -?-.

Opposite, below: Tewkesbury Cricket Club has been in existence since 1840 but this photograph records a feat very few ever achieve: Chris Attwell, on the left, is receiving a mounted cricket ball from the club president, Dr R.J. House at the AGM in the Tudor House Hotel around 1964. This was the ball with which Chris took all ten Cheltenham wickets at the Swilgate ground.

THE BELL BOWLING GREEN

MALLETT, PHOTO, TEWKESBURY.

The Bell Bowling Green, *c.* 1910. The club used this green until the mid-1970s when the new owner of the Bell Hotel wished to use the green for extending his hotel facilities. Tewkesbury Borough Council, together with the Tewkesbury Guild, raised sufficient funds to provide a new bowling green at the Vineyards, providing the club with a new clubhouse and purpose-built green. It is believed that the monks at the abbey used the old green.

Opposite, above: Another pub celebration, this time at the Black Bear, reputed to be the oldest pub in Gloucestershire. This was the winning darts team in around 1958. From left to right, back row: M. Sollis, L. Ingrams, Tim Colley, Mr Mace, Mr Wagstaff, -?- and landlord Norman Drew. Front row: ? Mace, C. Broughton, S. Mace, K. Curtis and G. Jordan.

Opposite, below: The Tewkesbury YMCA football team of 1960. The club has been involved in local football for upwards of 100 years, with varying degrees of success. From left to right, back row: T. King, R. Green, R. Sayers, H. Cartwright, A. Atwell, -?-, B. Goodwin, M. Beach, W. Salmon. Front row: G. Page, L. Stevings, R. Robinson, S. Goodwin, J. Sim.

1921 saw the Tewkesbury C of E Boys' School sports day held at the Swilgate ground. *The Cheltenham Chronicle* and *Gloucestershire Graphic* published this photograph on 2 July. In picture 2, headmaster Mr Ricketts checks the programme with spectators looking on. Picture 5 shows R. Green winning the Junior 100 yards race. A. Weaver wins the Middle School 100 yards event (picture 6) and T. Collins is successful in the Senior 440 yards race (picture 7).

In 1961, the Swifts Boys' Club were in their new headquarters at Canterbury Leys. To celebrate, boys challenged the mayor, Cllr H. Workman, to a tiddlywinks tournament!

A football team with one man short! This is the Swifts Boys' Club in 1965, at one of the many sporting activities they were involved in. From left to right, standing: –?–, ? Styles, P. Sayers, –?–, R. Lane and J. Perry. Kneeling: T. Drinkwater, B. Ricketts, D. Romeo, D. Hartell.

TEWKESBURY ABBEY CHOIR
FOOTBALL XI.

The winners of the hoseball competition pictured earlier, now more or less dried out. The prize, made by the firemen who organised the event, is crowned with a fireman's helmet. Extreme left: ? Smith. Second from left: A. Pryce Jones.

Opposite, above: Tewkesbury Cricket Club winning the Tewkesbury Hospital Cup in 1960, at the Swilgate ground. From left to right: A. Collins, M. Sollis, B. Devereux, A. Poole, -?-, G. Shephard, T. Crisp, P. Fox, C. Burd, D. Haines, K. Haines.

Opposite, below: The Abbey Choir football eleven looking pleased with themselves, around 1910. Regrettably there are no names to put to these sportsmen but the young man with the eyepatch looks particularly aggressive. Note the large leather football, typical of the game until the advent of the plastic-coated ball used today.

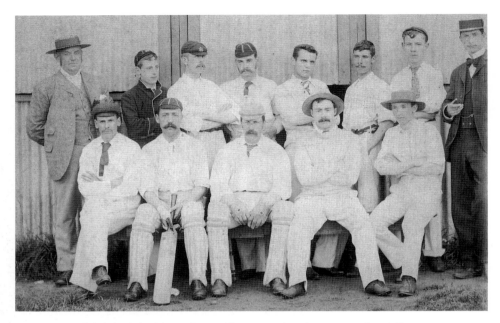

The cricket club, which had been formed by 1840, played at quite a few different venues before obtaining a permanent home in 1867 at the Swilgate. This is the earliest photograph of members, dated around 1880. From left to right, back row: A. Rix, ? Atkins, ? Wood, S.C. Mayall, ? Purnell, ? Lane, ? Graham, H. Hopkins (umpire). Front row: ? Harrison, C. Davis, W. Heath (captain), ? Gouldney, ? Fowler. The captain, W. Heath, was known locally as Whopper, from his enormous hitting.

These are the gentlemen bowlers of Tewkesbury in 1904, at the Bell Bowling Green, where the club played for many years. The club was one of the founder members of the County Bowls Association and was formed before 1830. The club are here on the green reputed to have been used by the monks of the abbey in medieval times. They have also played for some year some the Swilgate Cricket Ground, between the wars and have now moved to a new green at the Vineyards.

four

Events

In most towns there are innumerable events celebrating a variety of things, and most hoping to raise funds for good causes. Tewkesbury has been no different, with fêtes being held annually for the abbey and the local hospital, as well as many other organisations. In 1971, however, Tewkesbury rose to great heights in celebration of the anniversaries of the consecration of the abbey and the end of the Wars of the Roses, by organising events throughout the whole summer. Here are just a few.

In 1971, Her Majesty the Queen visited the town to present Maundy money to selected residents. A local artist, Arthur Bell, recorded the scene for Tewkesbury Abbey. His painting shows the procession from the choir down the aisle to present the small bags containing the coins. This was the first time the Queen had presented these gifts outside London.

The Coronation of King George V in 1911 brought many events, not only in this town but also all over the country. Parades, parties and dancing in the streets were the order of the day. Photographs were not permitted, by order of the council, but the *Tewkesbury Register and Gazette* produced a souvenir programme recording all the events for the princely sum of sixpence.

Below: Fêtes are a typical sight all over the country. This one was organised by the British Legion in 1960 raising funds for a worthy cause, and included a Hanging out the Washing Contest, an unusual one! The lady third from the left is Liz Boskett, and her husband, Jack, is on the right holding their son Brian.

The Tewkesbury Hospital Fête is an event that is held annually in the hospital grounds, with the aim of raising funds for specific purposes at the hospital. At the 1938 fête, the staff joined in, of course, and the old-style Matron, Miss Hutton, watched over the events of the day, as she did in the hospital. Local personalities Leonard Hone and Harry Hewitt gave their time voluntarily and the people, as they do now, supported the fête wholeheartedly.

Boatbuilding has a long history in Tewkesbury, as might be expected when the town has two major rivers. From punts, barges and sailing boats to MTBs (motor torpedo boats) for the Admiralty, almost every kind of boat has been built here. This is the National Boat Show at Earls Court in around 1965 and Bill Shakespeare is showing off his speedboat to Lord Snowdon. Bill broke the world water speed record in a boat of his own design; sadly he later died while practising to try and improve on his record.

The *Cheltenham Chronicle* and *Gloucestershire Graphic* were on hand in 1922 to record the official dedication of the war memorial to those who fell in the First World War. Mrs Didcote, who lost three sons in the conflict, unveiled the cross. The town council, in top hats, and many ex-servicemen attended the ceremony.

'DAILY MAIL' AEROPLANE FLIGHT OVER TEWKESBURY. 26TH JULY, 1912.

In the early part of the twentieth century, aeroplanes were still a marvel to be wondered at. In 1912, the *Daily Mail* organised an air race around England. The plane in the picture was piloted by a Mr Valentine, the eventual winner, seen here flying over the flour mills at the Mill Avon. The day after this flight, Col William Cody flew by and landed at Worcester.

Like most organisations in the town, the British Legion had its regular fête. This one was held in around 1955. The boy in the tub is Roger Wales, taking part in a competition in which the aim was to sit on a pole and balance without falling off. The small boy to the left of Roger looks like one of the Maycock twins, and on the right watching carefully is Roger Gee.

Vic Watson's garage in the High Street was a stopping point for a vintage car on a tour from Land's End to John O'Groats. The dress of the spectators indicates that the date was around 1948. Although the notice on the front of the car is indistinct, the car appears to be an early Wolseley.

The major attraction of this Tewkesbury Hospital Fête from around 1960 was the Ox Roast. The first cut was usually auctioned off by one of the celebrities attending and the chef was provided by the Army at Ashchurch camp, probably from the Officers' Mess.

Opposite, below: The Swifts Boys' Club provided the venue for this Christmas party in 1967. These are the young residents of Canterbury Leys. From left to right: Miss Roberts, Helen Jones, Ann Cook, Julie Wathen and Nicky Graham. Sitting opposite is Dean Graham.

In 1971, the whole town was involved in the summer festival and the Canterbury pub was no exception. They held a small fête in the grounds and here everyone is concentrating on the tortoise derby. The animal at the rear must have had a handicap! Included in the picture are Mr and Mrs Faulder, Bert Avery and Ted Keeper. The children include Nicola Graham and Nick Burd.

A collection for the Blind Association is being counted at the Berkeley Arms pub in Church Street in around 1968 and the customers are keeping a watching brief on the count. From left to right, standing: Mrs Wiggins, Mrs Cole, Bill Cole, -?-, Mr Wilkins, Mr Page, Mrs Turner, Mr Green, -?-, Mr L. Green and Mr Page. Seated: Mr Bevan, Ray Mulcock, -?- and -?-.

NATIONAL FEDERATION OF
DISCHARGED & DEMOBILISED SAILORS & SOLDIERS.

TEWKESBURY BRANCH.

= DRUMHEAD SERVICE, =

(In Memory of the Men of Tewkesbury who fell in the Great War)

HELD ON

SUNDAY, JULY 20TH, 1919.

ORDER OF SERVICE.

———o———

HYMN 1.

Tune—"*Lest we forget.*"

GOD of our fathers, known of old,
Lord of our far-flung battle-line,
Beneath Whose awful Hand we hold
Dominion over palm and pine—
Lord God of Hosts, be with us yet,
Lest we forget—lest we forget!

The tumult and the shouting dies;
The captains and the kings depart;
Still stands Thine ancient sacrifice,
An humble and a contrite heart.
Lord God of Hosts, be with us yet,
Lest we forget—lest we forget!

Far-called, our navies melt away;
On dune and headland sinks the fire;
Lo, all our pomp of yesterday
Is one with Nineveh and Tyre!
Judge of the nations, spare us yet,
Lest we forget—lest we forget!

If, drunk with sight of power, we loose
Wild tongues that have not Thee in awe
Such boastings as the Gentiles use,
Or lesser breeds without the Law—
Lord God of Hosts, be with us yet,
Lest we forget—lest we forget!

For heathen heart that puts her trust
In reeking tube and iron shard,
All valiant dust that builds on dust,
And guarding, calls not Thee to guard,
For frantic boast and foolish word—
Thy Mercy on Thy people, Lord! *Amen.*

PRAYERS offered by Rev. ERNEST F. SMITH, M.A., C.T.F., Vicar of Tewkesbury, & Honorary President of the Tewkesbury Branch N.F. of D. & D.S. & S.

HYMN 2.

Tune—"*Old Hundredth.*"

GREAT God, Who as in days of yore,
Art Prince of Peace and Lord of war,
Come forth! the whole round world awaits
The opening of Thy mercy gates.

Betwixt us and our Promised Land
New shapes of danger darkly stand;
'Tis not enough that war should cease,
Till from ourselves we find release.

Till human wills are made Divine,
No sun of righteousness can shine,
Nor any peace on earth begin
Till God has triumphed o'er man's sin.

Therefore, Thou King of all, come down;
Burn up our baseness with Love's frown;
Bid men by brothers' blood set free
Be brothers round one Calvary.

Or, if we turn not, teach again
The nations in new schools of pain,
Till from some dark chastising rod
Blossoms at last the Peace of God. *Amen.*

In 1919, the First World War had ended and people were beginning to give thanks and to recognise the servicemen and women who had served in the conflict. The National Federation of Discharged Servicemen organised a Drumhead service on 20 July 1919, which included the reading of a roll of honour of those who had lost their lives. Hymns were sung and the Last Post was played by Arthur Crockett of the King's Royal Rifles.

BOROUGH OF TEWKESBURY.

Sept.,
1939.

Aug.,
1945.

EX-SERVICE MEN & WOMENS

RE-UNION DINNER

TOWN HALL

SATURDAY, OCTOBER 26th, 1946

—

And doth not a Meeting like this make amends
For all the long years I've been wandering away?

Local businessman Sir George Dowty contributed a great deal to the life of the town, opening several engineering works and providing employment for the whole area for many years. Tewkesbury Council recognised these efforts by making him a Freeman of the Borough. This is a view of those attending the ceremony in 1959. On the front row are the councillors. From left to right: L. Webber, H. Workman, B. Sweet, Mr Troughton, Dr Holding, S. Walkley, L. Husband, Mr Hayward (chamberlain) and J. Turner (officer). In the audience are Lady Dowty, Mr and Mrs Robinson and Mrs Long.

Opposite: In 1946, a similar arrangement was made for those local ex-servicemen and women who had served in the Second World War. This time it took the form of a dinner and concert in the town hall on 26 October 1946. The mayor, Alderman H. Crouch, welcomed everyone and the Reveille was played by Mr Flowers. Vocalist H. Warner, comedian Chick Fowler and piano accordian players Messrs Wilkins and Jones provided the entertainment.

A St John's Ambulance Brigade dinner in 1964, with invited guests. At the top table, from left to right: S. Bick, -?-, Mayor L. Marsden, Mrs Bick, Dr G. Shephard, Mrs Shephard and R. Bishop.

Opposite, above: This is the official opening of the Swifts Boys' Club at Canterbury Leys in 1961. The mayor, H.Workman, looks on while chairman Martin Cadbury performs the official function. The club had been in several premises before this purpose-built structure was made available by the local council and county council funding. The building is now the Boys' Brigade headquarters.

Opposite, below: The audience have just enjoyed the first half of the Old Time Music Hall in the Watson Hall in 1970 and are now competing for the best fancy dress. The four men on the left are, from left to right: Cecil Graham, Ben Roope, C. Burd and Alan Wilkinson. The winner, being presented by the compère, is Derek Graham, who seems to be losing his moustache!

The Gloucestershire and Worcestershire branches of the English Folk Dance Society held their annual festival at Tewkesbury in July 1933. More than 600 dancers took part and, despite the rain, carried on dancing while spectators watched from under a variety of umbrellas. Dancers from a wide area took part, as well as the team from Tewkesbury Girls' High School.

Elections in the 1920s and 1930s were an important affair in the town, despite the fact that Tewkesbury and Cirencester formed one division. This election was perhaps considered important because the successful candidate, Mr Morrison, became the Speaker of the House of Commons. The tradition was that the winner spoke from the balcony of the Swan Hotel, after the result had been read out by the Under Sheriff for the County from the front of the town hall.

The Civic Society was a pressure group, formed after the demolition of the upper High Street in 1965, in order to keep a watching brief on the redevelopment of the town. It was started by the lady in the centre of this picture, Mrs P. Howells, who had worked for the government during the war. This is their annual dinner in 1967 and some of Mrs Howells' contacts are present. From left to right: Nicholas Ridley MP, Lady Dowty, Mayor G. Long, Mrs Howells, General Sir John Evetts, Miss Craighead and the Duke of Beaufort.

A parade to Tewkesbury Abbey to dedicate the new standard of the Tewkesbury branch of the British Legion took place in October 1930. Brigadier General Bainbridge DSO led the parade from the Cattle Market to the abbey and back through the town. The picture in the bottom right corner is of a group from the Sir William Rose lodge of the RAOB (Royal Antediluvian Order of Buffaloes), with the Primo W. Stone on the extreme right.

Opposite, above: The local Chamber of Commerce has been a strong organisation for many years, supporting trade and commerce in the town. Mr Ray Shill acted as secretary for some years and was also involved in many other local clubs and societies. In around 1970, the mayor of the town, Cllr L. Webber, presented the gift of a wristwatch to Mr Shill for his services.

An outing for the whole of the Tewkesbury Sunday schools in July 1933. The visit was to Denleys Gardens in Bishop's Cleeve, an extremely popular place for children. There were slides, swings and other attractions, as well as facilities for tea and snacks for the adults.

five

Trains and
Railways

The fascination of the steam railways is quite understandable: all that power, steam and noise create a magical sight for everyone, not just youngsters. The amazing fact is that the interest and fascination usually lasts a lifetime and the older the train or station, the more interest there is. Sadly, Tewkesbury no longer has a station; after having in the past not one but two, this is a blow to all enthusiasts. Here are a few memories of that age.

Above: This is the engine shed at the Maltings in Tewkesbury. The line on the right ran from the goods sidings across the High Street to the mills and the quay. In 1955, the buildings which would have been to the right of this view, Spring Gardens, had just been demolished, dating this picture around 1956.

Midland Railway Station. Tewkesbury

Tewkesbury station in 1913, showing the line from Ashchurch going north to Ripple and Malvern. Here you could buy your early morning papers from WHSmith, who had a shop on the station. A victim of the transport cuts which 'threw the baby out with the bathwater', the site is now derelict and a sanctuary for wildlife.

Opposite: The main line through Ashchurch went straight up north to Worcester and Birmingham, and this view, taken in 1957, shows the crossing which allowed the goods trains from the Tewkesbury line to cross to the east side of the station. Ashchurch station, which was closed in the late 1960s, has happily been reopened in the last few years, allowing access for passengers to the Midlands and the south.

The line to the original station on the High Street ran past the old malthouse and into the area containing the engine sheds. The large buildings to the right were converted into an engineering works for the Dowty Group but have since been demolished to allow the development of flats.

Looking down the line from the Chance Street crossing towards the station, one can imagine the gates across the line being operated to allow access for the train. We can just see some of the wagons parked beyond the house. These buildings – the gatekeeper's cottage and outbuildings – are gone now.

Another view of Tewkesbury station from around 1950, with the *Tewkesbury Bullet* standing by. On the opposite side of the track is the waiting room for the down line to Ashchurch. On the left, the driver and fireman appear to be having a quick smoke before setting off again.

A view of the engine shed from the High Street end of the line. To the right, No. 3754 stands under the canopy ready to take coal on board. The wall and properties on the extreme right are the line of terraced houses known as Spring Gardens. This dates the picture to around 1950, as the properties were demolished soon after that.

The site of the original railway station, which fronted onto the High Street, in around 1952. To the left we can see the remains of the old passenger platform and waiting room, with the original lamp still there. The roof over the station has gone and the site looks derelict. In the background, across Oldbury Road, is the large malthouse.

This is an earlier view, taken sometime in the 1930s, and shows the roof still over the station. The track is laid in stone setts, probably the original setts designed to give purchase to the wheels of horse-drawn carriages.

six
Schools

The earliest recorded school in Tewkesbury was for a group of boys taught in the abbey, with a teacher funded by a grant from Sir William Ferriers. This school later combined with Mr J. Priestley's Abbey School and became the Tewkesbury Grammar School. Other schools – the National, Trinity, Abbey Boys' and the Girls' High School – came along later, to be amalgamated under the new comprehensive system of education at a purpose-built school outside the town.

Here we have Tewkesbury Girls' High School, a misnomer really as the school took in boys as well. This is the Lower Fifth in 1930, with music mistress Miss Brasher in the centre. The school had a good academic record before it amalgamated with the other schools to form Tewkesbury Comprehensive School.

Opposite: In 1930, the Cheltenham Chronicle and Gloucestershire Graphic published a series of pictures called Tewkesbury Schools and Scholars, with a prize of 5s offered to the children whose picture was ringed. This one features Tewkesbury Grammar School and shows boys from the three houses: Ferrers (top), Clare (centre) and Neville (bottom). The grammar school started life at Abbey House in Church Street and later moved into purpose-built larger premises further along the street. Later, because of the high numbers, the school moved to a large property on Gloucester Road.

In 1882 the vicar of Tewkesbury, Hemming Robeson, founded the Tewkesbury High School for Girls at Avnonbrook House in Church Street. Originally a boarding school, which incidentally took boys as well, it became entirely a day school. In 1972, it closed and the pupils joined the grammar school boys at a new comprehensive school. This is the rear of the school taken in 1882 with a typical Victorian group of staff and pupils.

A different view of education in May 1927, with Tewkesbury Church of England School having won a competition run by the RSPB. The boys have all received medals and the Bird and Tree Challenge Shield. The top picture shows the committee members and some of the school staff, with the headmaster sitting on the extreme right. The names of the adults are printed but the boys go unnamed! Perhaps there were too many to list.

The Church of England Boys' School in 1933. The school was opened in 1911 and there were about 100 pupils. The teachers are of course long gone but there must be a great many students who still recognise themselves here.

Opposite, above: The Tewkesbury Grammar School speech day, held at Southwick Park in 1970, was a formal affair held in a substantial marquee. Parents were invited and speeches were made by prominent visitors. This was a school with an excellent academic record but it sadly went the way of almost all grammar schools, just a year after this picture was taken. The students in the front row include Stephen Sallis, Paul Burd and ? Keeper.

Opposite, below: Pupils at the Secondary Modern School in Chance Street, around 1946. It is winter judging by the cold appearance of the students. The boys have not yet got into long trousers and only a few girls wear gymslips.

This production of *Richard of Bordeaux* was a joint effort by Tewkesbury Girls' High School and Tewkesbury Boys' Grammar School and was performed at the Watson Hall in February 1959. Included in the cast were Richard Pitman, who later became a racing correspondent for the BBC, Colin Osborne, Peter Maycock, Diana Moses, Eileen Burke and Peter Raggett.

seven

Rivers and Weather

The location of the town alongside two major rivers has, of course, influenced the life of the town. These rivers and the small brooks around Tewkesbury have given a livelihood to the inhabitants for many centuries. Not only has boatbuilding been a prominent industry but also barge owners and bargehands abound in the list of occupations in census returns. The town is subject to flooding throughout the winter months and, as some of the pictures demonstrate, occasionally in the summer too. The incidence of such flooding appears to be increasing with the amount of new housing being built on the flood plain and may cause problems for future residents.

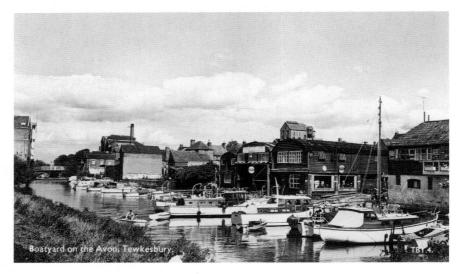

Above: The Mill Avon, around 1955, looking full of activity with boatyards and pleasure craft all along the river. This was the site of Bill Shakespeare's boatyard, which built racing craft that were sold worldwide. Bill himself was an avid sailor and broke the world water speed record on Lake Coniston. Sadly, he lost his life trying to improve the record.

Tewkesbury's Victoria Pleasure Gardens in 1897, seen from the Ham. The mayor, Cllr T.W. Moore, was present on this occasion, along with most of the town by the look of the crowd. The small island in the Avon has been used to erect patriotic flags, although it is not certain how long this would last in flood time. Later, a bandstand and a cannon were placed here as attractions.

42947. TEWKESBURY. VICTORIA GARDENS.

In this 1923 view of the Victoria Gardens, it is possible to see how the site has been developed. The bandstand has been built and during the summer the town band would play here. A popular place to walk on a summer's day and a secret meeting place for couples in the evenings, this was a typical piece of England.

Opposite, below: The river Severn in the 1930s with the town in the background. The steamer is towing several barges up the river, maybe delivering goods from the Borough Mills to Worcester.

A JUNE FLOOD 1924

One of Bathurst's steamers moored outside the Lower Lode Hotel in around 1910, waiting for the passengers to finish lunch at the hotel before moving on up the river. On the right, the ferry is transporting a pony and trap, which is probably travelling from Forthampton into Tewkesbury. This ferry had been in operation since medieval times. It belonged originally to the abbey and used to take the monks to their estates near Forthampton.

Opposite, above: Boatbuilding has been part of the history of Tewkesbury for many generations. C. Bathurst had his building works adjacent to King John's Bridge and enjoyed a great reputation for the quality of his boats. This photograph of the *Swallow* is taken from one of Bathurst's advertising booklets published in around 1910. He also had two major river steamers, which took parties up and down the rivers, and hired out skiffs and punts to the general public.

Opposite, below: A view of the inundation of June 1924 taken from Lower Lode Lane, where the two rivers meet. There was a ferry here for many years, taking passengers across to the Lower Lode Hotel or to Forthampton village beyond.

This view of the Severn looking upriver is an etching drawn by a Cheltenham printer, E. Burrows, in 1920. It was in this area that the Tewkesbury brickmakers had their businesses. Alongside the banks, they took out the clay to make Tewkesbury bricks. They were supplied to builders, not only in the town but to the surrounding district too. Tewkesbury bricks have been found in buildings all along the river towards Gloucester. In the background are the Malvern Hills and to the right the ground rises to the Tute.

eight

Miscellaneous

A watercolour drawing of Well Alley in the High Street, from around 1890. An unusual view, it shows the timber-framed buildings that were usual in most of the alleys. Well Alley was reputed to be the site of the first settlements, as there was a supply of spring water. The picture also shows the flow of water under one of the buildings, a view not seen in living memory.

The following group of pictures does not fit any specific category but is of sufficient interest to warrant inclusion in this book and will certainly jog a few memories.

This is the town hall on a typical Saturday morning, around 1938, with women waiting for the rummage sale to open. The sale was an attraction for local organisations trying to raise funds and for local people looking for a bargain. The lady at the back wearing a light dress is Mrs Bess Goode.

Floods in winter are the norm here; there are sometimes as many as five in the winter period. This one was unusual, being in June 1924. Mythe Road is deep in floodwater and, while the local lads were happy to watch the antics of the motor vehicles trying to get through, those with horses would be out making a few shillings pulling the less fortunate out of the causeway.

Spring Gardens was a row of three-storey terraced properties with communal toilets and washhouses facing them across a small garden. No en-suite facilities but a tin bath each Friday! The houses were situated on what is now the car park of the swimming pool and were demolished in 1955. This is No. 19 and the lady on the left is Jeannie (née Murphy) Walker, known as Irish Jinny, because she moved from Ireland in the late nineteenth century.

A couple of flappers? Not really – this is Mary Jean Walker (left), daughter of Jeannie, in around 1921. Mary Jean was born in Bank Alley and her father was a bargehand plying between Tewkesbury and Bristol. In 1920, these two moved to Birmingham for work and became barmaids. Mary Jean not only found work but a husband too and moved back to Tewkesbury shortly after, to live in Spring Gardens.

It would appear that noise pollution is not a new phenomenon. In 1915, the local authority decided to take action. This is a byelaw prohibiting the use of bells, gongs and other noisy instruments in any public place. It is possible that this is still a legal byelaw and as such could be enforced!

NOISY HAWKING.

No person shall for the purpose of hawking, selling, distributing, or advertising any article, shout, or use any bell, gong, or other noisy instrument in any street or public place in the Borough so as to cause annoyance to the inhabitants of the neighbourhood.

Given under the Corporate Seal of the Mayor, Aldermen, and Burgesses of the Borough of Tewkesbury.

Mayor.

Town Clerk.

A British Red Cross function just about to begin, around 1955, at one of the hotels in town. On the extreme left stands Mrs Carter and Miss Dyer is second from left. The gentleman is Mr Kirton, with Mrs Kirton beside him.

BYE-LAWS

in force for the regulation of

RAILS MEADOW :-

Horses and Carts, Cattle, &c., not to be brought into the Meadow.

Turf not to be cut or plants or trees injured.

Refuse or rubbish not to be deposited.

Throwing stones or other missiles is forbidden.

Carpets or mats not to be beaten or brushed in the Meadow.

Riotous or indecent behaviour, or indecent or obscene language is strictly prohibited.

Every person offending against any of the above Bye-Laws is liable for every such offence to a penalty of £5.

H. A. BADHAM,

TOWN CLERK.

The town council was in action again in 1922, issuing this byelaw with threats of fines. Rails Meadow was a piece of land alongside the Swilgate Brook and was once a play area for the children of the town. Now this once peaceful area is a car park operated by Tewkesbury Council and carrying a charge for motorists.

Constables Oath.

You shall well and truly serve our Sovereign Lord The King and The Bailiffs Burgesses and Commonalty of the Borough of Tewkesbury in the County of Gloucester, in the Office of a Constable man for the said Borough of Tewkesbury for One Year next ensuing or until You shall be thereof discharged according to due Course of Law: You shall well and truly do and execute all Things belonging to Your Office, according to the best of Your Knowledge,

So help You God.

The Victorian period was a great time for the giving and the taking of oaths. Bearing in mind some of the prosecutions reported in the police courts of the time, where short measure was a common occurence, this is not too surprising. This oath from around 1850 was taken by the locally employed constables. They promised to serve the King, bailiffs and burgesses for one year or until discharged.

Coalweighers Oath.

You and either of You shall swear that You shall well and truly serve our Sovereign Lord The King and the Bailiffs Burgesses and Commonalty of this Borough in the Office of a Coalweigher for the Year ensuing or until You shall be discharged of that Office by the Bailiffs and Burgesses or the Major part of them. You shall to the utmost of Your power do and execute every Thing appertaining to Your Office, honestly, justly indifferently and truly to the best of Your Skill and power,

So help You God.

An unusual oath of the same period was this one for coalweighers. It was a declaration to serve all and sundry and a promise to do everything appertaining to the office honestly, justly, indifferently and truly!

It is wartime and the RASC (Royal Army Service Corp) are in occupation at Ashchurch camp. This picture was taken at the Abbey Lawn in 1940 and includes a group of the lady volunteers who come forward at all these occasions to give their time freely.

Oyez! This is Ted Preston, the man who served as Town Crier in Tewkesbury for some three decades. He was Champion Crier of All England in the early 1950s and runner up on more than one occasion. He was a great ambassador for the town, visiting Canada, the USA and many other countries, for the town. Most of the work was voluntary, he received a small honorarium from the council and charged a small fee for 'crying' for other organisations.

The annual dinner of the Beckford Sand and Gravel Company in around 1964. This was an occasion when the company thanked its employees for a year's hard work. In the background is guest of honour, mayor Cllr L. Marsden. On the table nearest the camera are S. Walkley, Mrs Walkley, Tom Chambers and Doreen Chambers and other guests include H. Workman and his wife.

Trinity church in Oldbury Road has always had a large following from adults supporting the contingent of Boys' Brigade members at the church. This is a parish supper in around 1958. From left to right: Mrs Sweet, Bart Sweet, the head of the builder's and undertaker's opposite the church, –?–, Mrs Dickinson, Mrs Warburton, Mr Warburton and –?–.

One of the characters of the town, Jock Robertson, in around 1958. Jock was a barber who had his shop in Church Street. A Scotsman, he settled in Tewkesbury after serving in the forces during the Second World War. He worked from Monday to Saturday in his shop and on Sunday he would visit Tewkesbury Hospital and give haircuts and shaves to the patients in the men's ward.

The Hayward family have been ironmongers in Tewkesbury since 1820; the business has passed down through the family and is still thriving. This 1965 photograph was taken inside their shop. From left to right: Simon Hayward, Alec Hayward and Cecil Hayward, who was for some years chamberlain to the borough council. The whole family has a history of public service.

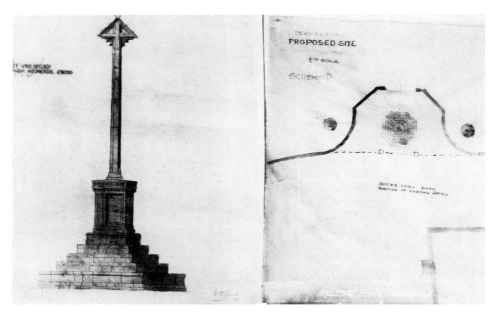

After the end of the First World War, towns and cities throughout the country honoured those who had been killed by erecting cenotaphs and memorial crosses. In Tewkesbury, a council committee and other interested groups were tasked with commissioning a design and finding a suitable site. This 1920 postcard shows one of three designs considered, together with a proposed site at the main gates of Tewkesbury Abbey. As we know, this design was unsuccessful, and the site was not used. The memorial was finally built at The Cross in 1922.

The restructuring of the High Street, which took place in the 1960s, initially created large gaps in the frontage of the main street. This was the area in 1967, before any building had taken place properly. The whole site is open down to the old Station Street and it is just possible to see the scaffolding being erected for some of the buildings. The large board shows that there were two supermarkets, nineteen shops and several flats planned for the site.

WELCOME TO O

nine

Pageants
and Festivals

Pageants have played a part in the life of the country since medieval times and Tewkesbury is no exception. There are records of passion plays and nativity plays in the abbey archives from that time. When life was hard and short, there was some small relief for the poor when they could witness dressing up and acting. In 1931, a pageant took place which is still remembered today and this was followed for a couple of years by musical and literary festivals based around the abbey. In 1971, a double celebration took place, not just for a few days but for several months, a major feat for such a small town. These are some of the records.

A name that is immediately recognised in the town is Gwen Lally, the producer of the Tewkesbury Pageant in 1931. This major event in the town took place from 14 July to 18 July in that year and ran at 3 p.m. and 7 p.m. on those days. The pageant is still strong in the recent history of the town, mainly because most of the residents were involved in one capacity or another. It was enacted on the meadows behind the abbey, now known as Pageant Meadow, and the list of patrons reads like Burke's Peerage. For a play that lasted just a few days, it made an enormous impact on the town.

The pageant included scenes showing the consecration of the abbey; the marriage of the two families who were supporters of the abbey, Beauchamp and Despenser; the Battle of Tewkesbury and the dissolution of the abbey. Photographs of the scenes appeared in a souvenir publication. This view shows a group on the meadow, with Abbot Parker performing the marriage ceremony between Lord Abergavenny and Isabel Le Despenser.

This is the scene depicting the Battle of Tewkesbury in 1471, with Prince Edward slain and the Lancastrian army defeated. Those taking part from the town made all their own weapons and armour; the chain mail consisted of knitted wool and the swords were made of wood for the sake of safety.

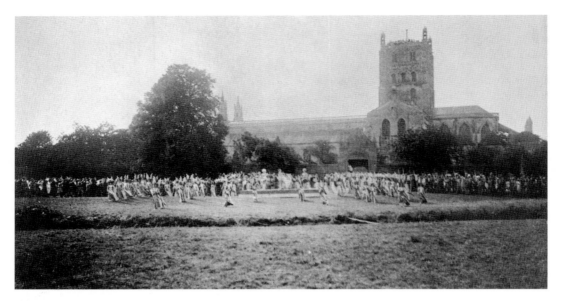

The Finale, with all the players assembled and arrayed around the centrepiece. Although seventy years have past, local people still speak fondly of the event.

Mrs Elizabeth Wyatt receiving her Maundy money during the ceremony in the abbey. The money was contained in small bags and the Queen passed down one side of the aisle and back up the other side. No names of recipients were given, as dealers would have been around trying to buy the coins.

Opposite, below: In 1971, Her Majesty Queen Elizabeth indicated that she would be happy to visit Tewkesbury to present Maundy money to selected elderly residents. The ceremony took place at Tewkesbury Abbey at Easter 1971 and the town took on an air of a festival. It was in fact the year of the festival commemorating the 500th anniversary of the Battle of Tewkesbury and the 750th anniversary of the consecration of the abbey and events of all kinds were played out throughout the summer months. This is a view of Church Street and the Queen walking toward the abbey to present the Maundy money, escorted by Mr P. Healing.

After the presentations and a pause for refreshments in Abbey House, Her Majesty went on the customary walkabout along Church Street and is seen here among the crowd at The Crescent.

1971 was also the year when the town was selected to take part in the BBC show *It's a Knockout* and were appointed to play against Hereford at Tewkesbury. A team of local sportsmen and a manager were selected from the town and, working to broad instructions for the games, the team practised at Ashchurch camp. There was a crowd of almost 20,000 people in attendance at the Vineyards. The results were very close but the town was victorious and were then approved to play in Rotterdam against continental teams. The team included Mjr Bill Davidson (extreme left), Town Crier Ted Preston (extreme right), Dave Hallings, Dave Heeks, Roger Allen and Frank Lewis (in dark glasses on the left).

Opposite, below: The Queen met those involved in the massive restoration programme which the long row of Abbey Cottages, which were originally medieval shops and merchants' properties, were undergoing at the time. The Abbey Lawn Trust undertook the restoration and the architect was Jeremy Benson. From left to right: a local solicitor, Phyllis Howells and Alec Mills.

Tewkesbury Festival Cricket Match

Lancashire v Yorkshire

Wednesday 21 July 1971 25p

In 1971, Tewkesbury Cricket Club played host to a replay of the Battle of Tewkesbury, with Lancashire playing against Yorkshire, but this time with just bat and ball. This was a unique match as it is still the only occasion that the two sides have ever played outside the two counties. A large crowd attended and the teams were entertained by the club after the match.

A ball was held to mark the 1971 celebrations in a marquee on the Abbey Lawn. Acker Bilk was the great attraction, playing with his Paramount Jazz Band to a sell-out audience of some 700 people. There was a turkey buffet dinner and all that goes with such a spread; it was a real celebration. The picture is of Acker and his band, with Cllr Derek Graham and his wife Maureen looking on.

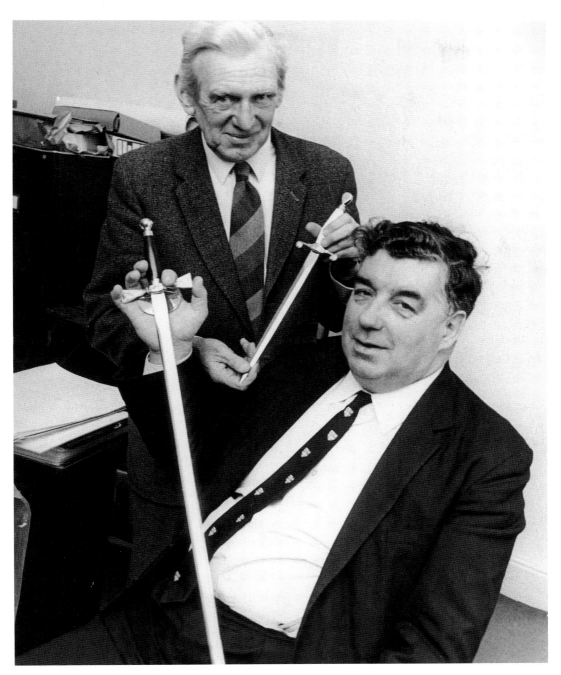

Mr George Wilkinson, who was at the time manager of Cheltenham Town Hall, took up the post of Organiser of the Festival. The council had considered organising these events with the officers they employed but soon realised that this was a major operation, not to be undertaken lightly. It would be difficult to overestimate the work done by Mr Wilkinson, bearing in mind the multitude and diversity of events, including the visit of the Queen. Here he is with a colleague, Mr Davis, showing off a sword and poignard made to commemorate the festival.

The mayor during this year was Cllr L. Webber, a blind physiotherapist working at Holme Hospital. His handicap did not prevent him from taking a full and active part in the whole year. He led the parade to Tewkesbury Abbey when the Queen attended and was able to present a Tewkesbury sword to the Duke of Edinburgh after the formal dinner at Tewkesbury School. Here he is being presented to Her Majesty by the Duke of Beaufort in full dress. Mrs Webber and Mrs Smale, wife of the Town Clerk, are looking on.

There were many feats to perform in the *It's a Knockout* competition. In this event, the competitors are trying to pass a medicine ball along a series of boards held high at arm's length. Some idea of the size of the crowd can be seen from this view of one side of the arena.

ten

Villages

There is a close association between Tewkesbury and the multitude of villages that surround the town. As they all lie within a few miles of the town and most of them fall within the administrative borough of Tewkesbury, the residents in the villages use the facilities in the town. The comprehensive school brings together the children aged eleven to eighteen, forming friendships that tend to knit the town and its environs together.

Woodroofe's Tea Rooms, Coombe-Hill.

This is Northway and the picture will be recognised as the present Northway Hotel. This photograph was taken in around 1946 and gives us some idea of how the area looked before the major housing estates were established. Part of this site is now taken up by a small supermarket and other shops.

Opposite, above: Dances were regularly held at Ashchurch army camp. These events were a major attraction, particularly for the local girls. Coaches would be run to and from the surrounding villages as well as Tewkesbury and the charge was 2s for a dance with a live band. This picture was taken in 1948 and at that time most of the soldiers were on National Service for eighteen months in REME (Royal Electrical and Mechanical Engineers) or ROAC (Royal Army Ordinance Corp). At the table with the soldiers is a NAAFI girl in uniform and on the right is Pauline Gibbard, a Tewkesbury girl.

Opposite, below: The small village of Coombe Hill lies just outside Tewkesbury. This is a true Edwardian scene, taken at a time when life was lived at a slower pace than today. There would have been this kind of tea rooms every few miles across the country, catering for the few who travelled by car and all those who were taking up the new craze of cycling. There were clubs for cyclists in most towns, including Tewkesbury, as it was a new and cheap form of travel and gave everyone a sense of freedom not felt before.

During the Second World War, a camp set aside for prisoners of war was built in the area around Northway. The inmates were not cooped up all day; some of them were let out in organised groups to local farmers to undertake jobs on the land. After the war, when the prisoners were sent back to Germany, local people – families waiting for housing to become available locally – occupied these huts. The complex formed a large village on its own, with a chapel and other facilities.

The chapel building in the camp was used, of course, by the prisoners but was taken over by the residents after the war. The huts in the background probably belong to the army camp just down the road from Northway.

Opposite, below: The camp was of considerable size and had many facilities. It was policed by the British Army and the fencing around the camp appears to be just a token restriction. Certainly, from local reports, the large number of prisoners were happy to be here and some were reluctant to return to a defeated homeland and perceived disgrace.

A sports day was organised internally and was a gala day for the prisoners. The winners of the various events are seen here receiving their prizes from the camp commandant, with a German aide alongside him.

Opposite, below: Aschurch camp has been a major employer of civilians since it was first built. After the REME and RAOC arrived, there were some 500 soldiers here. The workshops and stores were quite extensive and the MOD set up a training school for apprentices at the camp; there was a great deal of competition for places. This picture shows some of the civilians who have just received Safe Driving Awards from Maj. J. Gascott of the RAOC. Back row, fourth from left: Ron Allen. Front row, second from left: J. Liddell.

Out to Bushley, only a couple of miles away, and it is Christmas. Bushley is a small self-contained village with a great community spirit. This party from around 1959 took place in one of the village halls, probably attached to the church.

A little further from Tewkesbury is Bredon Village, which has grown somewhat from the time of this picture taken at the turn of the twentieth century. This is Corner Cottage at the junction of the road to Tewkesbury, on the left, and the road to the church and the Fox and Hounds pub, on the right. The cottage is still there and the land behind it is now developed with housing along the road to Tewkesbury.

Going past Ashchurch just a mile or so we come to Aston Cross, not exactly a village but still a close community. The place has sported a strong cricket club for many years, with a ground just off Ashchurch Road. This photograph was taken in around 1958 and includes Mrs Yates, who probably acted as scorer and did the teas as well, her husband Mr Yates, Fred Gibbs, Gil Gibbs, Ron Garfield, John Nation (in spectacles), Ray Mulcock, the umpire and local farmer Mr Hill.

Other local titles published by Tempus

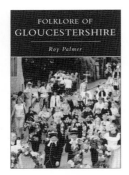

Folklore of Gloucestershire

ROY PALMER

Here are recounted tales inspired by landscape, village lore, legends, superstitions, stories of devils, fairies, witches and ghosts, sports and fairs, song and dance, revels and rituals. Roy Palmer is an acknowledged authority on the subject of folklore, and his work in collecting material from within the traditional boundaries of Gloucestershire is a major contribution to the historic records of the county.

0 7524 2246 4

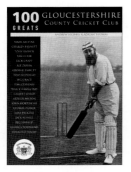

Gloucestershire County Cricket Club: 100 Greats

ANDREW HIGNELL AND ADRIAN THOMAS

Gloucestershire CCC are steeped in tradition, with the history of the West Country club being richly decorated with some of English cricket's most famous names. Indeed, none could be larger than Dr W.G. Grace. This book proudly recalls the generations of illustrious players who have represented Gloucestershire and built on the record-breaking achievements of the immortal Doctor.

0 7524 2416 5

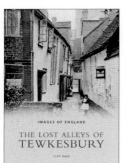

The Lost Alleys of Tewkesbury

CLIFF BURD

The lost alleys of Tewkesbury are a fascinating subject for research. Some carry the name of a pub, many are a reminder of families who lived there and others reflect the occupation of the residents. These alleys, the people who lived, worked and eventually died there, are the story of the town itself. They reflect its growth, its industry, its fortunes and misfortunes, and recreate a sense of Tewkesbury past.

0 7524 3189 7

Haunted Gloucester

EILEEN FRY AND ROSEMARY HARVEY

Gloucester's historic docks have some strange stories to tell and the city's twelfth-century cathedral also has its secrets. From a ghostly procession at Berkeley Castle to the Grey Lady at the old Theatre Royal, this new and fascinating collection of strange sightings and happenings in the city's streets, churches and public houses is sure to appeal to anyone intrigued by Gloucester's haunted heritage.

0 7524 3312 1

If you are interested in purchasing other books published by Tempus, or in case you have difficulty finding any Tempus books in your local bookshop, you can also place orders directly through our website

www.tempus-publishing.com